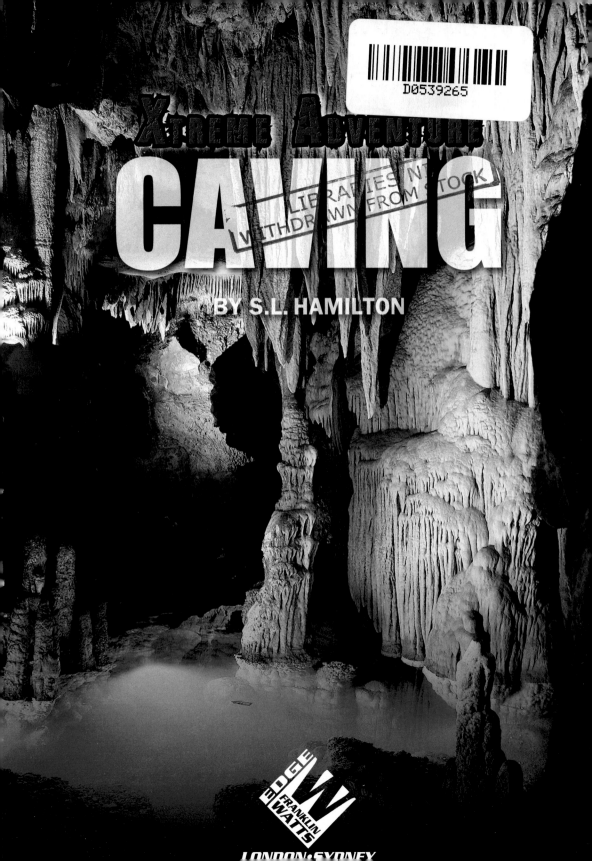

Xtreme Adventure
CAVING

BY S.L. HAMILTON

EDGE
FRANKLIN WATTS

LONDON·SYDNEY

This edition first published in 2015 by
Franklin Watts
338 Euston Road
London NW1 3BH

Franklin Watts Australia
Level 17/207 Kent Street
Sydney NSW 2000

Copyright © 2014 by Abdo Consulting Group, Inc.

First published in the USA by ABDO Publishing Company.

Editor: John Hamilton
Graphic Design: Sue Hamilton
Cover Design: Sue Hamilton

Acknowledgements:
Cover Photo: Getty Images.
Interior Photos: AlaskaStock-pgs 22 & 23; AP-pgs 10-11; Corbis-pgs 6-7, 16-17, 24 (inset)
& 27; Getty Images-pgs 8-9, 12-13, 14-15, 15 (inset), 20-21, 24-25, 29 (top & center);
Glow Images-pgs 4-5, 18-19, 21 & 29 (top inset); Lawrence Goldman-pg 21 (inset);
National Geographic-pg 32; National Park Service-pg 29 (bottom left and right); Ron
Niebrugge-pg 26; Thinkstock-pgs 1, 2-3, 28 (bottom left & second from left) & 30-31;
U.S. Geological Survey-pg 28 (bottom right); W.Tucker-pg 28 (bottom second from
right).

Every attempt has been made to clear copyright. Should there be any inadvertent
omission please apply to the publisher for rectification.

A CIP catalogue record for this book is available from the British Library.

Dewey Classification: 796.5'25

(HB) ISBN: 978 1 4451 3981 4
(Library ebook) ISBN: 978 1 4451 3984 5

Printed in China

Franklin Watts is a division of Hachette
Children's Books, an Hachette UK company.
www.hachette.co.uk

CONTENTS

CAVING

Cavers love the thrill of exploring underground worlds. But going into caves can be dangerous. Tight spaces, cold temperatures, slippery rocks and steep drops are common challenges. However, explorers often find beautiful formations, crystal-clear lakes, amazing waterfalls and unusual creatures. Caving is an extreme adventure!

XTREME FACT – Caving is also called potholing, speleology or spelunking.

CLOTHING & EQUIPMENT

Cavers wear a base layer of warm clothes covered by a two-piece wetsuit or a waterproof oversuit. On their feet they wear wool socks and strong leather or rubber boots. Sturdy leather gloves and knee pads are smart 'extras'. A harness or load-bearing belt is used to carry extra supplies.

XTREME FACT – Cavers carry either electric (battery-powered) or gas (acetylene) lamps. An electric lamp may work for up to 12 hours. A carbide lamp, which runs on acetylene gas, is lighter in weight, but works for a shorter time.

A helmet is very important. It protects an explorer's head. It is equipped with a light that allows a caver to keep both hands free.

Most equipment is simple. Ropes and ladders are the main equipment needed for caving. However, knowing how to place it and how to move safely into and through a cave takes skill and knowledge.

XTREME FACT – *Well-equipped cavers carry first-aid kits, survival bags, whistles for communication and at least one backup light source.*

Cavers must not only protect themselves,
but they must also protect the caves
they enter. Caves are fragile places.
Rock formations that took thousands
of years to create may be destroyed
in seconds.

DANGERS

Caving is a dangerous adventure. An explorer may suffer broken bones from a slip or fall and need to be rescued (below). Caves sometimes collapse. Falling rocks are always a danger. Rain outside the cave may cause flash flooding inside.

Cavers can die from drowning, freezing, falling, being crushed, and from getting lost or stuck inside a cave. Yet cavers are drawn to this extreme sport. They may see areas never before explored by another human being. It's an adventure they can't resist.

XTREME FACT – The most important caving rules are never go into a cave alone and always tell someone your planned route and when you expect to return.

LIMESTONE CAVES

Limestone caves are usually formed by rocks being worn away by groundwater. It is estimated that 90 per cent of caves in the world are limestone caves. The Mammoth Cave in Kentucky, USA, is by far the longest limestone cave in the world.

The Green River carved out Mammoth Cave's wide passageways, narrow tunnels and gigantic domed rooms. Only about 644 km of Mammoth Cave has been explored. It is estimated that the cave may be more than 1,609 km long.

Mammoth Cave is part of the United States National Park system. Several kilometres of the cave are explored each year. Visitors may take tours of explored areas.

Krubera Cave in the Western Caucasus is the deepest known limestone cave in the world. It is over 2,191 m deep.

Lechuguilla Cave (lech-uh-gee-uh) in the USA is known for its amazing gypsum stalactite formations (below).

Experienced cavers continue to explore and map Lechuguilla Cave's many passageways.

XTREME FACT – Lechuguilla Cave was formed by sulphuric acid bubbling up from the ground and mixing with water to dissolve the limestone from the bottom up.

SANDSTONE CAVES

Sandstone caves are created by wind and water erosion. Many are not very deep. Sandstone caves sometimes form in deserts and cliffs, such as those found in Australia and the American Southwest (below).

XTREME FACT – Ancient people, such as some of the Anasazi, lived in sandstone caves in Nevada's Valley of Fire and Colorado's Mesa Verde.

In the Table Mountain area of South Africa there are over 50 different sandstone caves. The largest of these is the Wynberg Cave system. It is extremely dangerous because of the deep holes in the cave floor.

LAVA TUBE CAVES

Lava tube caves form when a volcano's lava flow cools from the outside. If the inside remains molten, the material may flow out, leaving behind a hollow tube. These caves have formations made from the dripping and splashing of lava.

Well-known lava tube caves are found in Iceland, South Korea and Hawaii. Kazumura Cave (below), on Hawaii's Big Island, is more than 60 km long. It was discovered in the mid-1990s and is one of the longest lava tube caves in the world.

SEA CAVES

Sea caves are also known as littoral caves. They are found along coastlines where waves strike weak points in the rocks and erosion occurs. Sea caves are small in size, and are usually reached by boat or kayak. Many explorers go in when the tide goes out. Cavers must keep track of the water levels so they are not trapped inside.

XTREME FACT – The longest littoral cave is Painted Cave, off the coast of California, USA. It is 366 m long – tiny by limestone cave standards – but huge for a sea cave. Painted Cave got its name because of the rocks, lichens and algae that make it look so colourful.

Painted Cave

ICE & GLACIER CAVES

An ice cave is any type of cave that has some ice in it all year long. Cavers exploring the below-freezing cold zone look for icicles, ice columns, ice-stalagmites, needle ice, frozen waterfalls and ponded water, which is surface water that has frozen into a clear mass.

A glacier cave is a cave made entirely of ice. It is created when meltwater runs through a glacier and wears away enough ice to form a cave and passageways inside. Mendenhall Glacier near Juneau, Alaska, has an ice cave. Shapes and colours vary, but it is often a world of blues and whites.

Boots with crampons, ice axes and gloves are needed to explore ice caves.

Sinkholes & Cenotes

Sinkholes are deep holes in the ground. If the sinkhole is filled with water, it is called a cenote (seh-NOH-tay), which is Spanish for 'natural well'. Sinkholes and cenotes form when the ground collapses. The collapse may be caused by a cave falling in on itself or by man-made changes to the ground, such as mines or broken water pipes.

An aerial view of sinkholes and cenotes in Mexico.

Sinkholes are entered via ropes. Cavers dive into cenotes. They wear diving gear to explore these underwater caves. Many feel that these are some of the most beautiful caving experiences.

MUD & BOULDER CAVES

Mud caves are rare. They form when water erodes a narrow channel in the rock.

The channel fills in from landslides. Later, additional floodwaters erode the lower debris and leave behind a muddy cave. Anza Borrego State Park in California, USA, is known for its mud caves.

Boulder caves are also known as talus caves. They are openings underneath and behind a stack of boulders. Boulders stack up after a rockslide. Water running in and around the boulders wears away the soft earth and creates a cave.

FORMATIONS & CAVE LIFE

Most caves have some type of stalactite or stalagmite formations. There are also some rare discoveries. 'Popcorn', 'bacon', 'pearls' and 'parachutes' are just a few of the unusual and delicate formations found in caves. There are also mammals, amphibians, crustaceans and arachnids that only live in caves. Cavers are careful to explore, map and photograph while protecting a cave and its wildlife.

Popcorn
Formation

Bacon
Formation

Cave
Pearls

Parachute
Shield

*Mexican Free-Tailed Bats,
Carlsbad Caverns, New Mexico*

*The Olm (cave lizard),
Dinaric Alps, south east Europe*

*Cave Crayfish,
Mammoth Cave,
Kentucky*

*Harvestman,
Cuchillo Cura,
Argentina*

29

GLOSSARY

ANASAZI
Ancient Native American people, some of whom once lived in sandstone caves in the southwestern United States.

ARACHNIDS
A class of living things that includes spiders and scorpions.

CAVE FORMATIONS
A unique form, such as a stalactite or stalagmite, created by minerals being deposited within a cave.

CRAMPON
A metal plate with sharp spikes that attaches to boots. Crampons are used by cavers and mountaineers to walk on ice without slipping.

GLACIER
An immense sheet of ice. Melting and dripping water may create a cave within the frozen ice sheet.

GROUNDWATER
Water that collects underground in soil and between rocks.

STALACTITES

An icicle-like formation that hangs from the ceiling of a cave. It is formed from the mineral calcite being left behind as water drips down from above.

STALAGMITES

A pointed formation that grows up from the ground of a cave. It is created as calcite-rich water drips down from a cave's roof, deposits on the floor and builds upward.

TALUS CAVE

Another name for a boulder cave. Talus caves form when rocks drop down into a pile and openings are worn away under the rocks.

INDEX